Sweet Surprises
Accidental Food Inventions

by Jennifer Monaghan

NATIONAL
GEOGRAPHIC
LEARNING

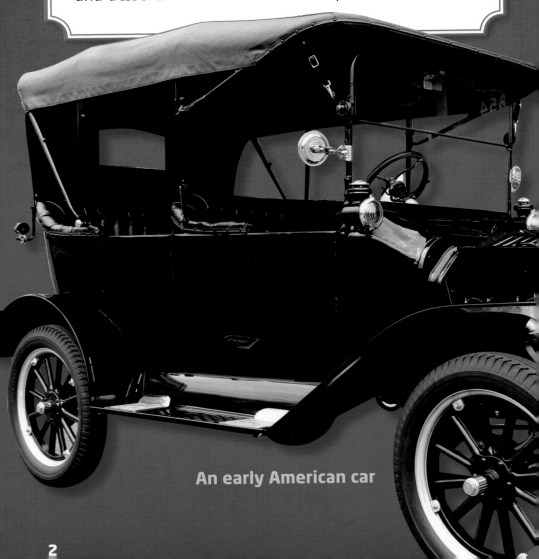

Some inventions are created on purpose. Their inventors work hard to create them. The light bulb, the television and the car are examples of these types of inventions.

But, some inventions are created by accident. Their inventors don't know they are creating something until they see the invention. Some popular snacks and desserts were invented this way.

An early American car

An early television

An early light bulb

Chocolate Chip Cookies

In 1930, a woman called Ruth Wakefield owned a small hotel with her husband. Ruth used to bake chocolate biscuits for the guests. But one day, Ruth had a problem. She hadn't got any cocoa powder for her biscuits.

Ruth came up with a solution. She broke a bar of chocolate into lots of small pieces. Then she put the chocolate pieces into the dough.

Ruth expected the pieces of chocolate to melt and make the biscuits chocolatey. But the pieces didn't melt. Instead of making chocolate biscuits, she made chocolate chip cookies!

Ruth agreed to let the chocolate company put her recipe on their boxes of chocolate. In return, the company gave her free chocolate for life.

Ruth Wakefield

Today, chocolate chip cookies are one of the USA's favourite treats!

Crisps

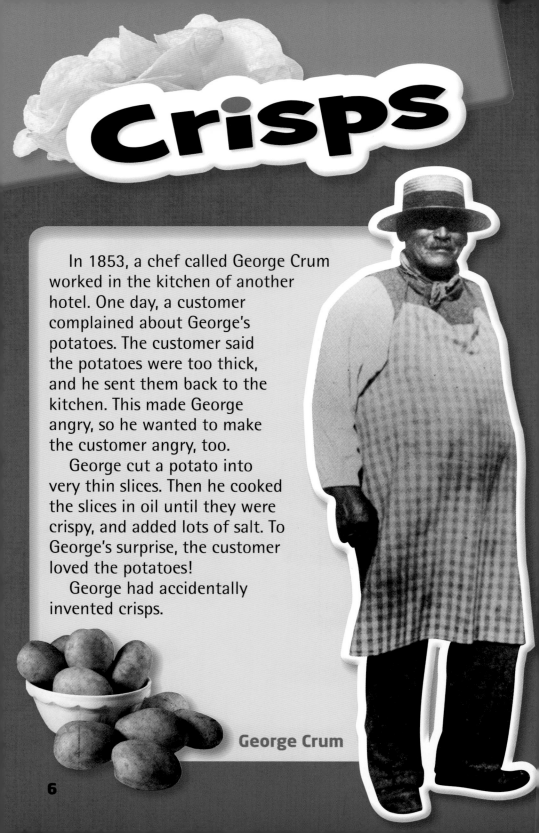

In 1853, a chef called George Crum worked in the kitchen of another hotel. One day, a customer complained about George's potatoes. The customer said the potatoes were too thick, and he sent them back to the kitchen. This made George angry, so he wanted to make the customer angry, too.

George cut a potato into very thin slices. Then he cooked the slices in oil until they were crispy, and added lots of salt. To George's surprise, the customer loved the potatoes!

George had accidentally invented crisps.

George Crum

Today, people all over the world eat millions of packets of crisps every year.

Ice Lollies

In the early 1900s, children used to drink fizzy drinks made from mixing sparkling water and fruit-flavoured powder. One day, an eleven-year-old boy called Frank Epperson stirred his drink with a wooden stick, then left the drink outside. It was very cold that night. The next morning, Frank found that his drink had frozen on the stick. Frank had accidentally made the first ice lolly.

Eighteen years later, Frank remembered his frozen treat. He started a business selling it and became very successful.

Frank Epperson

Today, about 3 million ice lollies are sold each year, and you can buy them in more than thirty flavours.

Ice-Cream Cones

In 1904, there was a big fair in the United States called the St Louis World's Fair. A man called Ernest Hamwi was selling thin Persian waffles at the fair. Nearby, another man was selling ice cream.

It was a hot summer's day. People bought a lot of ice cream. Soon the ice cream seller ran out of cups.

Ernest used his creativity to solve this problem. He rolled a waffle into a cone and put a scoop of ice cream in it. Some say this was the first ice-cream cone. People loved it!

The St Louis World's Fair in 1904

Remember, some wonderful inventions were created by accident. You never know what an accident can lead to.
So next time you do something by accident, ask yourself: 'Is there a good idea in this accident?'

11

Facts About Another Invention

As you've read, some popular foods were created by accident. But did you know that a popular device for cooking foods was also invented by accident?

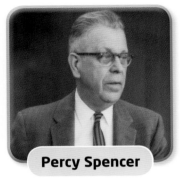

Percy Spencer

A scientist named Percy Spencer invented the microwave in 1945. Percy worked with radars. Radars use radio waves to find the location of things such as boats and aeroplanes. During World War II, they were used to help find enemy aeroplanes.

One day, Percy was working with a machine that makes radio waves. Suddenly, he noticed that the chocolate bar in his pocket had melted. This gave him an idea. Maybe radio waves could heat food.

Percy tried another experiment. He used the radio waves on popcorn kernels. The popcorn kernels popped! He used the radio waves on an egg. The hot egg exploded all over Percy's colleague.

By accident, Percy had invented the microwave.

The first microwaves weighed 350 kilograms (about 770 pounds) and were 1.8 metres (6 feet) tall! Of course, microwaves are much smaller today and are used in millions of homes around the world.

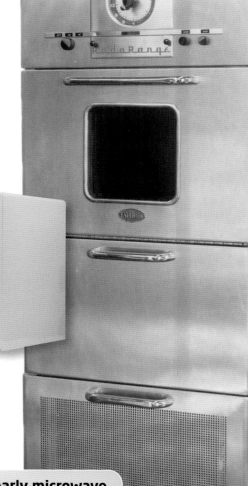

A modern microwave

An early microwave

Fun with Creativity

Unscramble the words to complete the sentences.

invent   problem   solution   idea   creativity

ttiviyraec

1. This child used his _creativity_ to make a car out of a box.

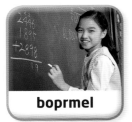

boprmel

2. This child is trying to solve a _____.

vtneni

3. This child likes to _____ new things.

diae

4. An invention can start with a creative _____.

noostiul

5. Sometimes, it is easy to find the _____ to a problem.

Draw a line from each problem to its solution.

Problem

Solution

Think of a problem you've had recently. What solution did you find for this problem? Write a few sentences about the problem and your solution. Use a bilingual dictionary if necessary.

Glossary

accident something that happens in a very unusual or surprising way

crispy firm but easily broken

device a thing made to do a particular task

expect think that something is likely to happen

fair

fair an event, usually outside, with fun activities and things to buy

frozen turned solid by very cold temperatures

guests people staying in a hotel or another person's home for a short time

melt

melt to change from a solid to a liquid usually because of heat

powder

powder a dry dust made of very small pieces

recipe a set of instructions for making a food dish

snack food eaten between meals